You and Me: We're OPPOSITES

Published by Scholastic Inc.,
557 Broadway, New York, NY 10012,
by arrangement with Blue Apple Books c/o
Chronicle Books LLC. SCHOLASTIC and associated
logos are trademarks and/or registered trademarks of
Scholastic Inc.

12 11 10 9 8 7 6 5 4 3   11 12 13 14 15/0

Printed in the U.S.A.   40

First Scholastic printing, September 2010

by **Harriet Ziefert**

illustrated by **Ethan Long**

You and Me: **We're OPPOSITES**

SCHOLASTIC INC.
New York Toronto London Auckland
Sydney Mexico City New Delhi Hong Kong

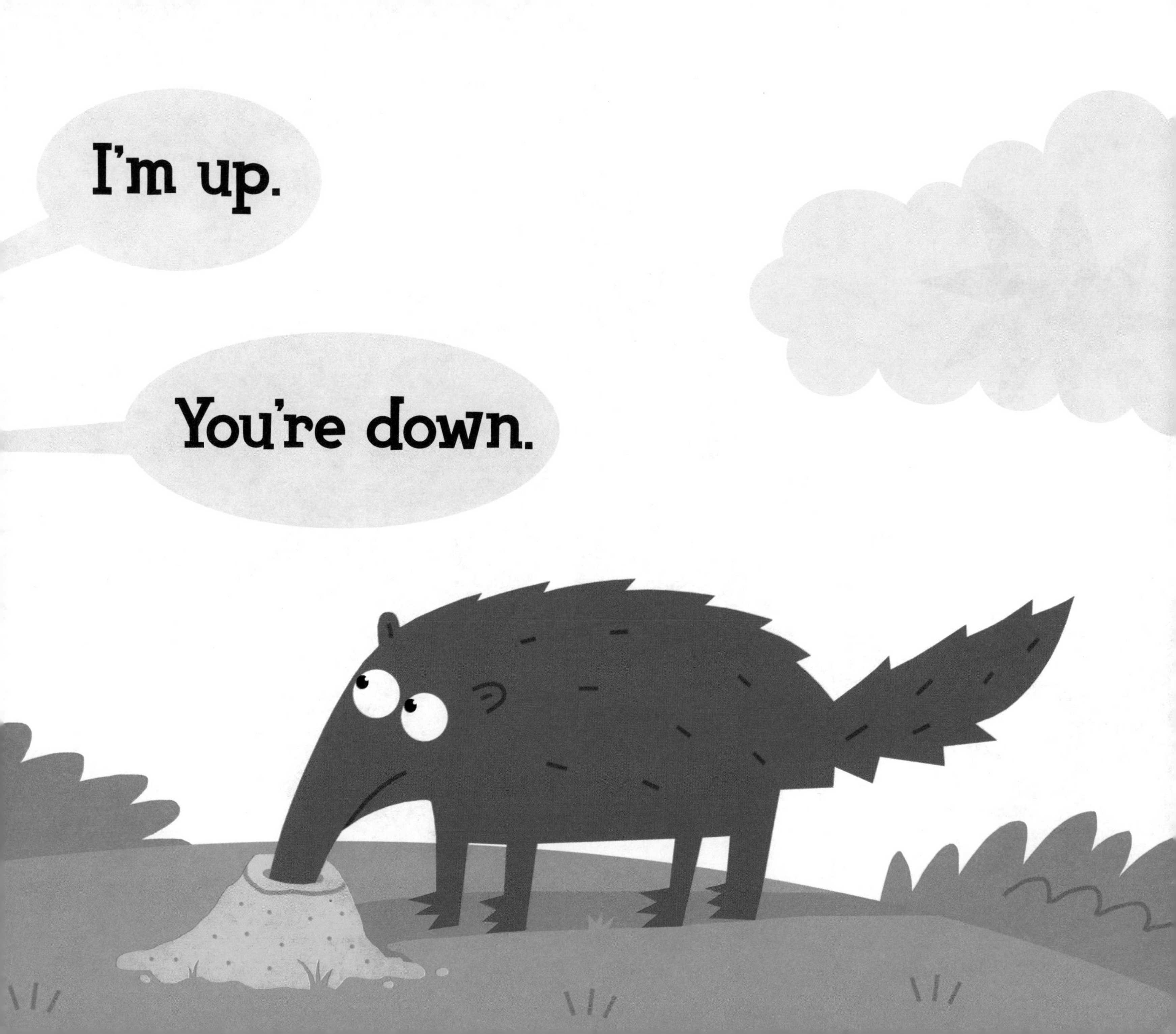
I'm up.
You're down.

I'm big.

You're little.

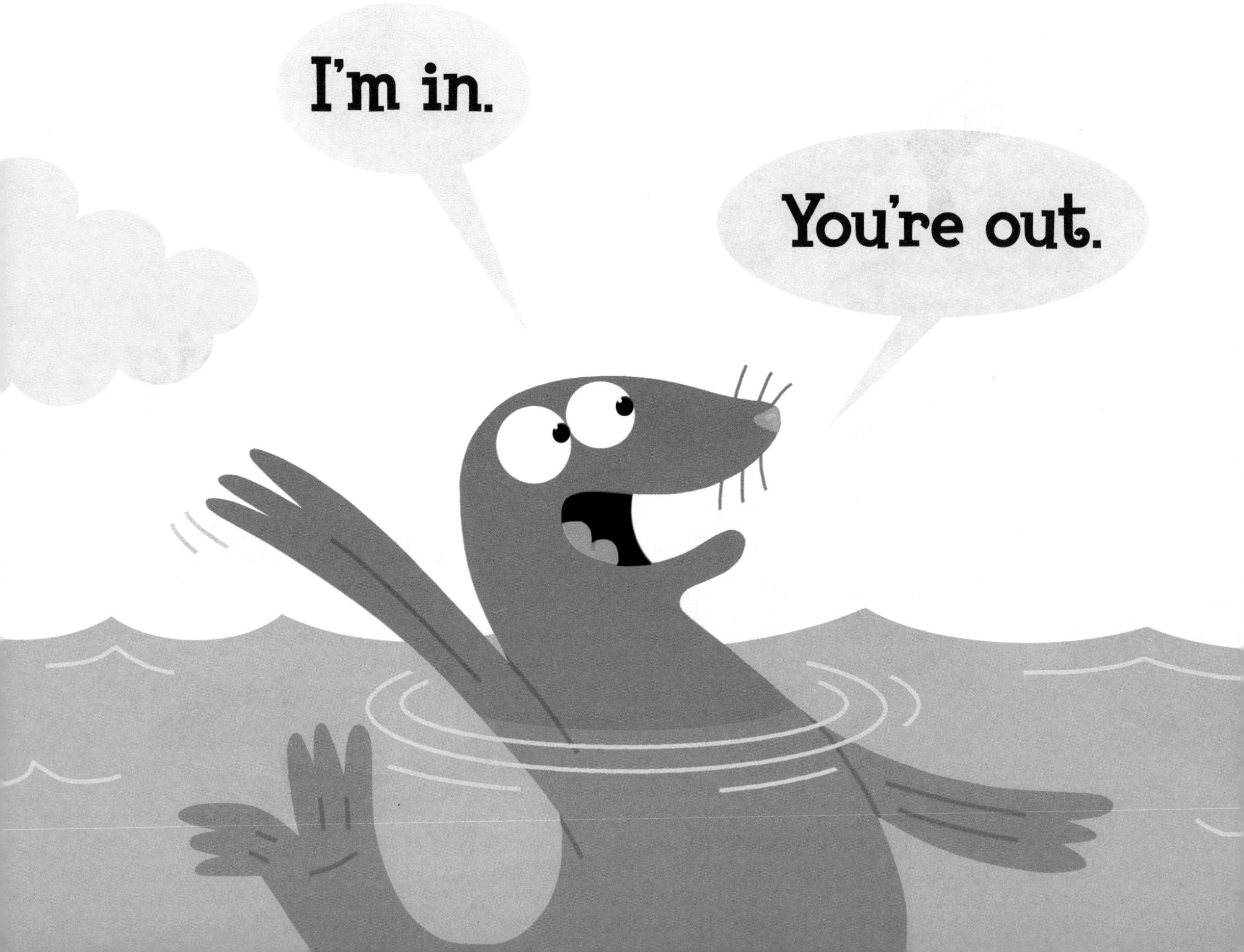
I'm in.
You're out.

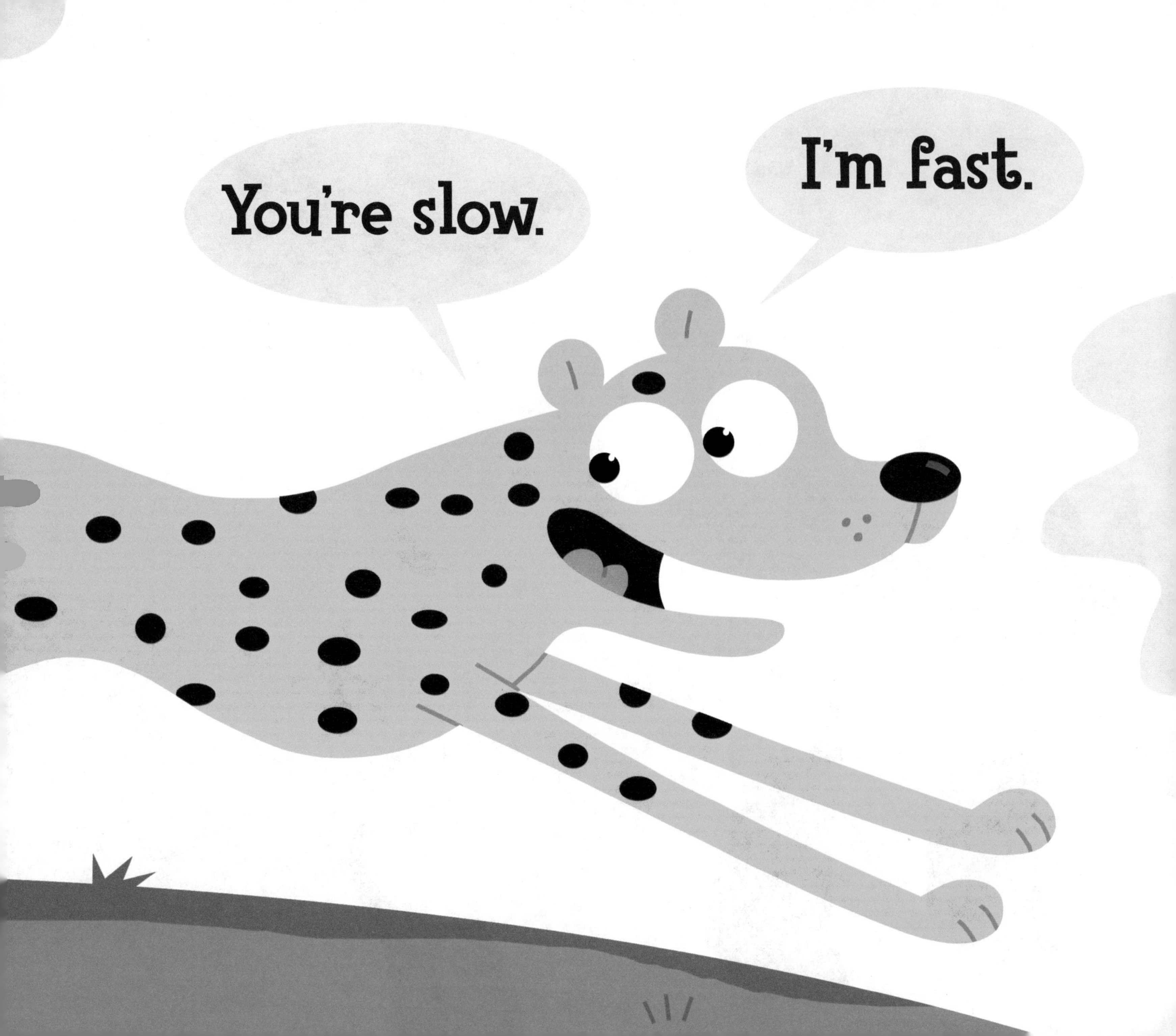
I'm fast.
You're slow.

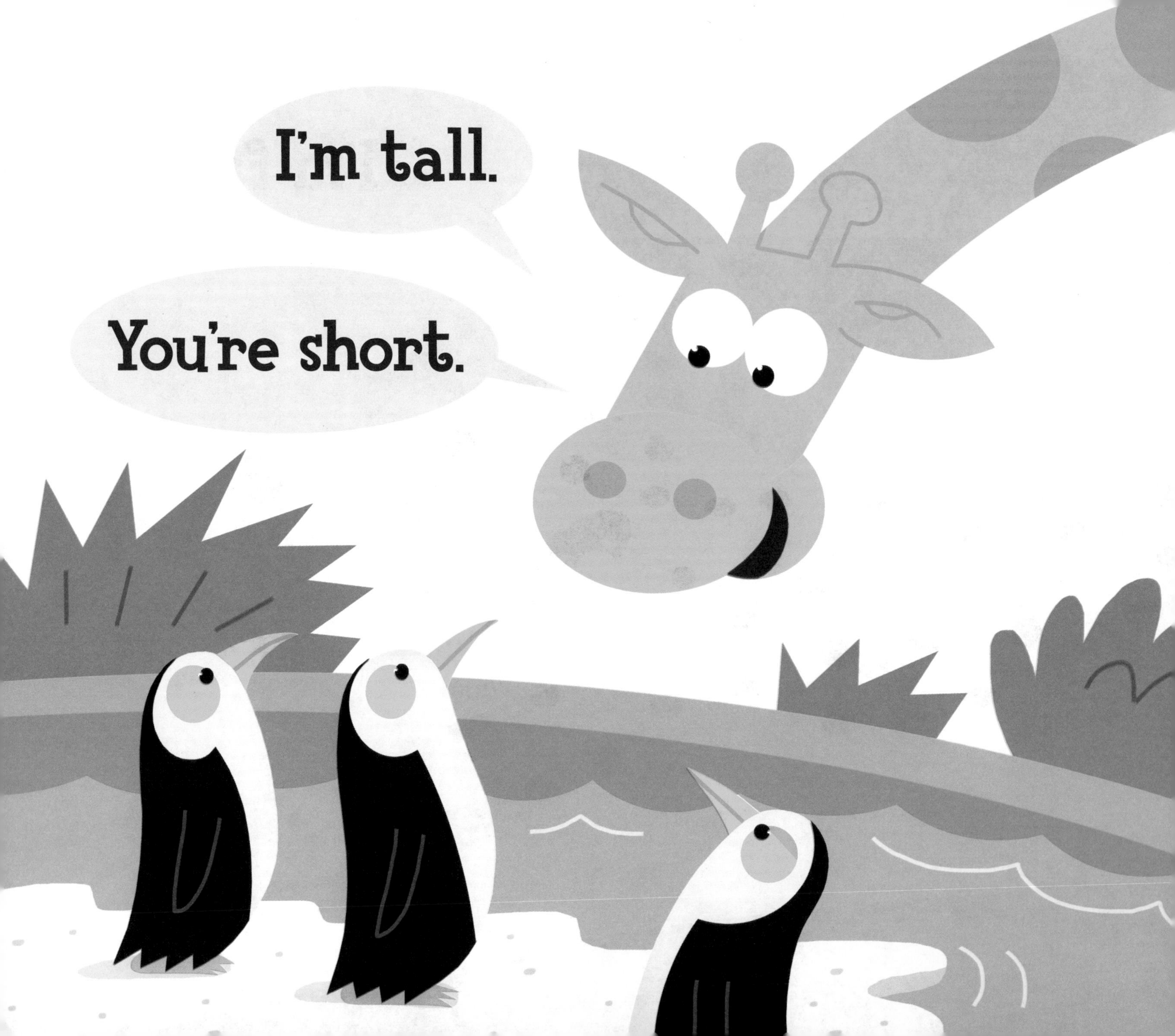
I'm tall.
You're short.